Who Is
Stacey Abrams?

Who Is
Stacey Abrams?

by Shelia P. Moses

illustrated by Dede Putra

Penguin Workshop

For my oldest sister,
Barbara Moses Lucas—SPM

PENGUIN WORKSHOP
An imprint of Penguin Random House LLC, New York

First published in the United States of America by Penguin Workshop,
an imprint of Penguin Random House LLC, New York, 2022

Visit us online at penguinrandomhouse.com.

Library of Congress Cataloging-in-Publication Data is available.

Printed in the United States of America

ISBN 9780593519721 (paperback)   10 9 8 7 6 5 4 3 2 1 WOR
ISBN 9780593519738 (library binding)   10 9 8 7 6 5 4 3 2 1 WOR

Contents

2020 Girl Scouts of Greater New York

Who Is Stacey Abrams?

In 2020, Stacey Abrams was invited to speak at the Women of Distinction Breakfast that was held by the Girl Scouts of Greater New York. During her virtual speech, she talked about the legacy of Juliette Gordon Low (the founder of the Girl Scouts) and her idea that young girls are the "makers" of history. Stacey said that Girl Scouts "gather the principles of speaking truth to power." But what does that mean? Speaking truth to power can mean calling out injustice, demanding change, and courageously speaking up for what's right—especially to people in authority or those who have political power. Stacey Abrams—who had once been a Girl Scout herself—took this idea very seriously.

Stacey went on to say that Girl Scouts are

dedicated to leading lives of service and justice. And Stacey is living proof of that. She had joined protests as a college student, became a lawyer to better understand the rights of all people, and helped create laws to protect them.

In her speech, she also talked about how Girl Scouts do so much more than earn the badges you see on their uniforms. They volunteer in their communities and work hard to serve others. And this is very true of Stacey. She wanted to make sure people in her community in Georgia had the opportunity to register to vote in future elections, including the 2020 presidential election. During this time, as a champion of voting rights, she often spoke to young people about the importance of using their voices—and their votes—to fight for change. Stacey did not know it then, but her dedication to serving others was about to leave an enormous mark on the entire nation.

CHAPTER 1
The Road to Georgia

Stacey Abrams was born on December 9, 1973, in Madison, Wisconsin—a state that, at the time, did not have a large population of Black people. The first Black person to live in Madison was an enslaved woman who was brought there in 1839 by the person who enslaved her, James Morrison.

The Black population had not grown much a century and a half later when Stacey's parents, Robert and Carolyn, moved to Madison from their hometown of Hattiesburg, Mississippi. The high-school sweethearts had only been back in Hattiesburg a few years, after graduating from college, when Carolyn Abrams was accepted at the University of Wisconsin–Madison

(UW–Madison). The young couple was very excited about Carolyn being able to earn her master of library science degree at UW–Madison. After the move, Stacey's father worked hard to take care of his growing family while his wife finished school.

Stacey—the second-oldest child—and her sister Leslie both were very small when their mother fulfilled her dream of becoming a librarian. In 1977, Stacey's parents decided to move to Gulfport, Mississippi, after Carolyn got a job as a librarian at William Carey College. Sometimes the children went with their mother to work. They had to keep quiet, so they would sit on the floor and read. Their home was also filled with books for the children to read. They enjoyed reading the World Book Encyclopedia.

When Stacey's father arrived home from his job at the shipyard, the Abrams family gathered around the television after dinner. They frequently watched an educational television station called the Public Broadcasting Service (PBS), so Stacey and her siblings were able to keep up with current events, politics, Black culture, and other cultures around the world.

Although both parents worked very hard and their family was never without food, they were often short on money and needed to take on extra jobs to earn more. In addition to his regular job, Robert cut tree limbs for neighbors and cleaned parking lots for local businesses. At one point, Carolyn and Robert managed their aunt's restaurant. Over the next few years, the Abramses welcomed two sons, Walter and Richard, along with a daughter, Andrea, to their family.

Robert and Carolyn insisted that their children do three things: go to church, go to school, and take care of one another. All the children, who said they were best friends, were very smart and made good grades, but when it was time to play, Stacey was different. While her sisters and brothers liked running around outside, she would

sit inside reading books. She loved speaking at church and at school. Stacey entered several spelling bees, and she was very proud when she won in the sixth grade.

Even though the Abrams children were great students, Carolyn and Robert knew that having a good education did not mean that white people would see them as equals. In the United States, Black people and other minorities were not being treated fairly simply because of the

color of their skin. But Stacey's parents believed that voting was a sure way for them and other Black people to be heard and to make changes in their communities. They often brought their children with them to the polls so they could witness their parents voting. And despite having money for only their essential needs, the family always found ways to serve people who had less than they did. They would make trips to prisons to participate in outreach programs and donated food to homeless shelters. Stacey's parents would encourage the children to work in soup kitchens where free food was given to those who could not afford to buy it. These trips helped to shape Stacey's life before she was old enough to realize it.

When Stacey was in high school, the Abramses moved to Atlanta, Georgia, so that Robert and Carolyn could attend Emory University. Both parents were now students at the seminary school to learn more about the Bible, God, and the Methodist religion, in preparation for becoming ministers. Now that her parents were in school, the entire house was filled with students.

Stacey was an excellent student at Avondale

High School. Along with her sisters and brothers, she continued to be a devoted reader. Stacey had also become interested in writing. While still in high school, she landed a job as a typist for a congressional campaign. She was very excited to work for a candidate who could possibly become a member of Congress and help make laws for the nation. The staff was so impressed with the edits Stacey made to a speech she was typing, they offered her a job as a speechwriter when she was only seventeen years old.

In 1991, Stacey graduated, and her parents looked on proudly as she gave her speech as the first Black valedictorian—the student with the highest grades in the graduating class—in the school's history!

The family was thrilled when they learned that all Georgia valedictorians were invited to a reception with Governor Zell Miller. They beamed with joy as they rode the bus to the beautiful Governor's Mansion, which is located in the wealthy area of Atlanta known as Buckhead. Their happy moment was nearly ruined when a guard at the gate tried to turn them away because he assumed a young Black woman would not be the valedictorian for her class. The staff apologized, but it left a bad memory in the minds of the Abrams family, especially young Stacey.

"I don't remember meeting the Governor of Georgia. . . . The only thing I remember is a man blocking the gates . . . telling me that I did not belong."

CHAPTER 2
College Years

In the fall of 1991, Stacey entered Spelman College, a Historically Black College or University (HBCU) for women, in Atlanta, Georgia. She majored in interdisciplinary studies, which included courses in political science, economics, and sociology. Like her parents, Stacey was interested in equal rights and social justice, so she became very involved in student government during her freshman year. Because she was determined to make a difference in college, she cofounded a group called Students for African American Empowerment.

Earlier that year, Stacey and other Black Americans were outraged when they learned that an unarmed Black man named Rodney King had been badly beaten by white police officers while they were trying to arrest him in Los Angeles, California. When on April 29, 1992, four of the police officers were put on trial and found innocent of any wrongdoing, riots broke out in Los Angeles and across the country.

The students from the Atlanta University Center, which includes Spelman College and other colleges and universities, walked out of class in a protest led by Stacey and other student government leaders. People from the housing projects across the street joined the student protest, and a few fights broke out as the Atlanta police were sent to the campus by Mayor Maynard Jackson. The police blocked off all entrances to the campus, and tear gas was used to end the protest. Stacey was very upset that the news reported false stories about the students, so she attended a town-hall meeting and expressed her concerns to Mayor Jackson.

The protest on campus and her willingness to express her concerns directly to Mayor Jackson was the beginning of Stacey Abrams's journey to what Congressman John Lewis referred to as getting into "good trouble." He meant that when something isn't right, or fair, people must speak up and do something about it.

In June 1992, when Stacey was eighteen, she and other students joined the citizens of Georgia in their latest fight for equal rights. They were demanding that the Confederate battle flag symbol be removed from the state flag because it represents hatred of people of color, specifically Black people. Although it was only a part of the Georgia state flag, this battle flag was used by the Southern army during the Civil War as they fought to hold on to the system of slavery. There were many politicians and citizens in Georgia who felt differently and refused to change the state flag that had been adopted in 1956. Stacey and the other students from the Atlanta University Center decided to take action.

Even though it was raining, Stacey helped lead the 1.7 mile march to the capitol building to state their position. The students were face-to-face with Atlanta police officers who were dressed in full riot gear. Next to the police officers were agents from the Georgia Bureau of Investigation. The agents were taking more pictures than the press in their attempt to scare the students. The cameras flashed as the students burned a state flag on the steps of the Georgia State Capitol. The flames were not put out by law enforcement but instead by the rain. Only then did Stacey and her friends walk back to campus.

Stacey devoted a lot of attention to her work as an activist, but she continued to get top grades the entire time she was a student at Spelman College.

John Lewis (1940–2020)

John Robert Lewis was born near the town of Troy in Pike County, Alabama. As a child, he dreamed of growing up to be a preacher.

While in college at Fisk University, John joined an organization called Student Nonviolent

Coordinating Committee (SNCC), a group that marched for the civil rights of Black Americans. By 1963, he was in charge of SNCC and would go on to participate in many of the important moments in the civil rights movement, including the March on Washington at the Lincoln Memorial (where he was the youngest person to speak on stage) and the march from Selma to Montgomery in Alabama in 1965, where he and other marchers were badly beaten.

John continued fighting for justice throughout the rest of his life, even when it put him in danger. He was elected to the US Congress in 1986, where he served from 1987 until his death in 2020.

She was also a working student, and she spent one summer employed as a youth services intern for Mayor Maynard Jackson, whom she had questioned about the police releasing tear gas on students during the campus protest. Stacey also worked as an intern at the United States Environmental Protection Agency.

While attending Spelman College, she won the election for student government president. Her new role as president gave her the ability to reach more students at meetings and during her speeches. Serving as president also made Stacey realize that she wanted to be a politician one day. She hoped to make the kind of changes her parents had dreamed of for the Abrams children.

In May 1995, she graduated magna cum laude—with high honors—with a bachelor of arts degree and received a scholarship to attend the University of Texas at Austin, where she earned a master of public affairs degree in 1998. While working on her master's degree, Stacey entered law school at Yale University.

While making straight A's and working part-time, Stacey also fulfilled another dream: to become an author. In her third year of law school, she wrote a book called *Rules of Engagement*, a romantic thriller that would be published two years later under her pen name, Selena Montgomery. *Rules of Engagement* was just the start of her writing career.

In 1999, Stacey graduated with her juris doctor (law) degree from Yale Law School.

CHAPTER 3
The Lawyer and Politician

Although Stacey enjoyed being an author, she did not plan on writing full-time. Instead, she accepted a job at a law firm in Atlanta. She worked on cases involving health care and public finance. The young lawyer did not see this position as just a job but also as a way to serve her community.

In 2002, at age twenty-nine, Stacey left her job and was appointed by Mayor Shirley Franklin to work for the City of Atlanta as deputy city attorney, advising the city on matters regarding taxes, business, and sometimes lawsuits against the city. Her interest in politics was growing, and she had learned Mayor Jackson's and Mayor Franklin's styles of management, communicating, and helping the community. Even though Stacey liked working at the Mayor's Office, she knew that the best way to serve the people she so desperately wanted to help was to leave her position and hold public office.

In 2006, Georgia State Representative JoAnn McClinton made the announcement that she would not seek reelection, leaving the door open for Stacey to run as a Democratic Party candidate in the eighty-ninth district. Many people doubted she could win because she was new to politics. But Stacey won the election against her opponents, George Maddox and Dexter Porter, with 51 percent of the vote. She was on her way to the Georgia State Capitol, where she had protested the state flag years earlier.

Stacey was appointed to the appropriations, ethics, judiciary non-civil, rules, and ways and means committees during her first four years as a state representative. When she was elected as the minority leader for Georgia House Democrats in 2010, Stacey worked with the Republican governor, Nathan Deal, to reform the HOPE scholarship program to make sure it could continue providing money to students to pay for college.

In 2013, Stacey also created a nonprofit organization called the New Georgia Project. This voter-registration organization helped to complete over eighty-six thousand voter applications in 2014, which meant registering close to sixty-nine thousand new voters for the

Stacey watches Nathan Deal sign the HOPE bill, 2011

state. And they were mostly people of color. Newly registered voters meant the state of Georgia would have many more of its citizens going to the polls on Election Day.

In a very short period, Stacey had made a huge impact on voting rights and education for the citizens of Georgia. What people didn't know was that while trying to establish a way for young people to be able to afford a better education, Stacey was struggling to pay her own student loans.

CHAPTER 4
The Race for Governor

In 2017, with the support of her family, Stacey decided that she would like to run for governor. On August 25, she resigned from the Georgia House of Representatives to focus on her campaign.

Soon, voters were referring to the Democratic Party primary race as the "Battle of the Staceys" because Stacey Evans, another Black woman and House representative, was also a candidate. As the race became closer, the fact that Stacey Abrams was in debt was leaked to the press. Stacey boldly admitted that she had unpaid student loans as well as tax and credit card debts. She refused to let this attempt to embarrass her cause her to drop out of the race. Instead, she wrote an article for *Fortune* magazine and said, "I am in debt, but I am not alone."

Stacey released her tax records and her plans to pay the money she owed. As the attacks grew, her brothers and sisters remained what they had always been, her best friends, as they stood up for Stacey. Her honesty worked! Instead of criticism, Georgia citizens understood her situation because many were facing similar struggles, and support for Stacey grew.

After winning the Democratic primary race on May 22, 2018, Stacey became the first Black woman in United States history to be nominated for governor. She received endorsements from many high-profile people like President Barack Obama, Senator Bernie Sanders, and television personality Oprah Winfrey, but she also had the support of the people of Georgia. She was happy to receive their endorsements, but Stacey knew she had to work hard to win.

President Barack Obama at a rally for Stacey, 2018

It was reported that she visited every county in the state of Georgia except one during her campaign, no matter how tired she was.

Back at home in Hattiesburg, her parents hosted a fundraiser for their daughter. They also traveled to Atlanta and joined Stacey on the campaign trail. Her brothers and sisters had their own busy schedules, but they, too, campaigned for their sister.

On November 2, 2018, Stacey lost the race to Georgia secretary of state Brian Kemp by only fifty thousand votes. Stacey and many Georgians thought it was unfair for Brian to oversee his own election. She pointed out that Brian was able to keep voter turnout low by not allowing nearly 670,000 people to vote, even though they had tried to register. Brian was also accused of putting on hold over fifty-three thousand pending voter-registration applications. By doing so, over fifty-three thousand Georgians were not allowed to vote.

After all the votes had been counted ten days later, Stacey decided not to take any legal action against the state of Georgia and Brian Kemp. Many people in the media criticized her for not congratulating the new governor when she thanked her supporters after the race. But Stacey felt that if she congratulated Kemp, she would be overlooking problems that many people had with his decisions concerning voter eligibility.

She ignored the criticism and figured out a way to address voter suppression in future elections in Georgia. Voter suppression is an attempt to change the outcome of an election by not allowing or making it more difficult for some people to vote. Examples of voter suppression are enforcing strict voter-identification laws and trying to eliminate early voting and mail-in ballots. The groups most affected are people of color, the elderly, and people with disabilities.

THE ATLANTA PRESS CLUB INC.

Stacey Abrams debates Brian Kemp during governor's race, 2018

Stacey quickly announced her Fair Fight Action organization. The new organization's mission was to expose and reverse voter suppression, educate citizens about elections, and help ensure fair voting practices around the country.

CHAPTER 5
The Comeback

Even after losing the election for governor, there was no way to dim Stacey Abrams's light. Politicians, including then senate minority leader Chuck Schumer, encouraged her to put in a bid to become a senator, but she declined. She did accept his invitation to become the first Black woman to speak after a State of the Union Address. On February 5, 2019, she also became the first person not holding a government office to do so since the tradition began in 1966.

After Brian Kemp's election, Stacey was determined to make sure the citizens of Georgia never had to doubt the outcome of an election again.

She turned her attention back to the Fair Fight Action organization. Donations poured in, including five million dollars from former New York mayor Mike Bloomberg. Stacey began going door-to-door to encourage the elderly to vote.

She reached out to eighteen-year-olds who would be voting for the first time, and she talked to voters who had not yet decided who they would be voting for in the 2020 presidential election.

Other politicians, including then presidential candidate Joe Biden, saw the effect she had on voters, and they wanted to work with Stacey. She was under consideration to be Joe's running mate for vice president during the 2020 presidential election. Senator Kamala Harris was eventually selected for the role, but Stacey would go on to play a big part in the outcome of the election.

In August 2020, Stacey was one of seventeen speakers at the Democratic National Convention in Milwaukee, Wisconsin. She received a standing ovation. No one doubted that Stacey's Fair Fight Action was instrumental in helping to register thousands of voters in Georgia.

People around the country waited anxiously on election night—November 3, 2020—and a few days later, they watched the state of Georgia give its vote to a Democratic presidential candidate for the first time since 1992. It was noted that eight hundred thousand of the voters from Georgia had been registered by the Fair Fight Action organization.

The big win in Georgia helped Joe Biden become the forty-sixth president of the United States of America. Not only had Fair Fight Action helped the president to win, but Georgia Democrats Jon Ossoff and Raphael Warnock became US senators and gave Democrats control of the United States Senate. Fair Fight Action continues to help secure fair elections in the state of Georgia and around the country.

Even as she remained very active in politics, Stacey continued to write books. Her first legal

thriller, titled *While Justice Sleeps*, was released in May 2021 under her real name. Stacey has also written two nonfiction *New York Times* best

sellers. And she wrote a children's book about her love for reading and spelling titled *Stacey's Extraordinary Words.*

Stacey's hard work and service to others earned her a 2021 nomination for the Nobel Peace Prize, which is given to people whose contributions have benefited humankind. People including Presidents Barack Obama, Jimmy Carter, and Nelson Mandela and Dr. Martin Luther King Jr. have received this very special award.

On December 1, 2021, Stacey announced she was entering the race for governor of Georgia for the second time. The teenager who was turned away from the Governor's Mansion as a valedictorian refused to give up. The book lover, who eventually wrote her own books and helped win the election for the president of the United States, stepped back into the spotlight with no fear!

Timeline of Stacey Abrams's Life

1973 — Stacey Abrams is born on December 9 in Madison, Wisconsin

1977 — Moves to Gulfport, Mississippi

1991 — Graduates as valedictorian from Avondale High School in Atlanta, Georgia

1992 — Joins protest to remove the Confederate battle flag symbol from the Georgia state flag

1995 — Graduates from Spelman College

1999 — Writes her first romantic thriller novel and graduates from Yale Law School

2002 — Becomes deputy city attorney for Atlanta

2007 — Becomes a member of the Georgia House of Representatives

2010 — Becomes the minority leader of the George House of Representatives

2013 — Creates the New Georgia Project, a voter-registration nonprofit organization

2018 — Wins Democratic primary nomination for governor of Georgia, the first Black woman in history to do so

— Founds Fair Fight Action organization

2019 — Responds to the State of the Union Address on February 5

2021 — Nominated for Nobel Peace Prize

Timeline of the World

1972 — Shirley Chisholm, the first Black woman to be elected to the US Congress, runs for president of the United States

1974 — Baseball player Hank Aaron hits his 715th home run, breaking Babe Ruth's record

1976 — Negro History Week, created in 1926, becomes Black History Month

1977 — The first Star Wars movie is released

1983 — President Ronald Reagan signs a bill creating the annual holiday that commemorates Dr. Martin Luther King Jr.'s birthday

1992 — Mae Jemison becomes the first Black woman to go into space

1999 — Michael Jordan retires from basketball after playing for thirteen seasons and winning six National Basketball Association (NBA) championship rings

2005 — Condoleezza Rice becomes first Black female secretary of state in the United States

2008 — Barack Obama is elected the forty-fourth president of the United States

2018 — Marvel movie *Black Panther* opens in theaters worldwide

2020 — Coronavirus disease COVID-19 spreads globally

— Kamala Harris is elected as the first woman and woman of color to serve as vice president of the United States

Bibliography

*Books for young readers

Abrams, Stacey. *Minority Leader: How to Lead from the Outside and Make Real Change*. New York: Henry Holt and Company, 2018.

Abrams, Stacey. *Our Time Is Now*. New York: Picador Paper, 2021.

*Abrams, Stacey. *Stacey's Extraordinary Words*. New York: HarperCollins, 2021.

Merica, Dan, and Michael Warren. "Stacey Abrams Announces She's Running for Governor of Georgia," *CNN*, December 1, 2021. https://www.cnn.com/2021/12/01/politics/stacey-abrams-georgia-governor-race/index.html.

MSNBC. "Stacey Abrams: Recounts Are Schemes Designed to Perpetuate Big Lie." May 25, 2021. YouTube video, 8:06. https://www.youtube.com/watch?v=k4kLa4VvBJw.

Salzer, James. Stacey Abrams' Voting Rights Non-Profit Raised $51 Million in 2020," *The Atlanta Journal-Constitution*, November 17, 2021. https://www.ajc.com/politics/stacey-abrams-voting-rights-non-profit-raised-51-million-in-2020/UUMMMFIG2NF7HJNQP5U66ZWYF4.

The View. "Stacey Abrams Discusses Georgia's 2022 Gubernatorial Election." January 5, 2022. YouTube video, 7:08. https://www.youtube.com/watch?v=v_NvtjYfIyI.

YOUR HEADQUARTERS FOR HISTORY

Activities, Mad Libs, and sidesplitting jokes!
Discover the Who HQ books beyond the biographies